Action Books
Notre Dame, Indiana
2007

lobo de labio | lip

labio | wolf

Laura Solórzano | Translated
by Jen Hofer

Action Books

Joyelle McSweeney and Johannes Göransson, Editors

Jesper Göransson, Art Director

Kristina Sigler, Assistant Editor

John Dermot Woods, Web Editor and Design

Action Books gratefully acknowledges the generosity of the University of Notre Dame in supporting our mission as a press.

Thanks also to Cuadernos de filodecaballos for permission to reprint *lobo de labio*.

Action Books

Department of English

University of Notre Dame

356 O'Shaughnessy Hall

Notre Dame, IN 46556-5639

Learn more about us at www.actionbooks.org.

Introduction

I'm fretwork you say when you read me?
Yours are fauces that don't frequent my fruit.
—Laura Solórzano

I give it to you with fog against your tongue/so your head might hum

In September 2000, I began a publishing project called *Hoja Frugal* (*The Frugal Page*),[1] a poetry broadside like a single-sheet publicity flyer, printed in an edition of 4000 and given away for free on the streets of this border. Two months later, in response to the *Hoja*, a Word file from Guadalajara came into my possession: it contained the book *lobo de labio*, sent for our editorial board to consider. Laura Solórzano was a poet entirely unknown to me, and I must admit I had been feeling somewhat disillusioned with Mexican poetry written by women, since in general it tends to utilize the erotic as a revolutionary element or an avant-garde pretension, without contributing anything whatsoever to an exploration of language.

Days later, merely to be respectful as an editor (something equally entirely unknown to Laura) in response to a gesture of participation on the part of any author, I decided to sit down to read Laura's book, with the idea that I might make a selection to publish in the *Hoja*.

lobo de labio initially captured me with its phonetic content: a rhythmic fluidity produced by the alliterative links led my *subconscious* on a pleasurable journey until one line stopped me in my tracks:

> ...te doy con la bruma en la lengua
> para que tu cabeza cante...

> ...I give it to you with fog against your tongue
> so your head might hum...

I instantly flung the book away, with something like awe-struck terror: **who is this woman?**

After pondering the intellectual abyss implied by a line of that magnitude (a line from the poem "(dissections of the bridge)") and after walking around and around my room attempting to locate the root of what had transformed inside me with that single line; after attempting to capture the profound meaning of that short phrase, pointing on the one hand toward an inducement into musicality via a blow, and at the same time to making a gift of the obstacle fog generates (cold, cloud, visual obstruction, confusion), proffered to a highly sensitive organ, the tongue; after contemplating the mental hum that follows pain and the obstacle that carries also a sensual implication, and also the placement of the word "hum" beside "might" in an ambiguous construction: the imperative and inductive connotations which for me implied, basically: *I am conscious that through my dark side I am going to make you think* — I decided that I had to meet Laura Solórzano in person.

Using as my excuse a conference focusing on independent "writing workshops," I bought a ticket to Guadalajara solely to ascertain whether the writer of *lobo de labio* was actually alive. In Guadalajara, I found that: Laura is very much alive; she's a visual artist, a psychologist (though she does not practice), and the mother of three children; and at that time she was forty years old, a fact which locates her among a generation of poets who had already published and distributed at least two books nationally, and who currently tend to make their living as public officials in Mexico's ministries of culture.

Despite the structure of machismo within which official support of the arts in Mexico functions, and which affected Laura directly, in 1999 she published her second book on a very small scale (one hundred copies only) with the independent press Rimbaud, edited by the painter Rafael Cázares. Excerpts from the book, titled *Semilla de Ficus* (*Seed of the Ficus*), were selected by the poet and translator Jen Hofer to form part of the anthology *Sin puertas visibles: An Anthology of Contemporary Poetry by Mexican Women*. Without Laura's having sought or even particularly noticed it, her work began to be distributed more widely, and she began to be situated as one of the most highly-esteemed "marginalized" Mexican poets, surpassing the prestige of her contemporaries due to her rigor with words, and due also to the charged meanings that sustain her work as well as her challenging and even risky linguistic contributions.

Tension and Equilibrium

As I said earlier, the phrase that made me fling the book away and begin pacing in thought forced me to pause and linger inside the enormous charge of meaning and unity that exists in *lobo de labio*: though each poem is titled as if it were an independent entity, and in fact single poems can be extracted from the book to form complete units without the need for proximity to the other texts, *lobo de labio* is a book of poetry and not a collection of poems; it is a book with its own door and latch. *lobo de labio* thus becomes a place, a place constructed out of language, a mental time the author puts forth to give refuge to her most intimate depths, the reflection of the structure of a thought in a sole unique instant, and not merely a sequence of anecdotes, as tends to happen in more traditional contemporary poetry.

Laura uses the apprehensions of the *subconscious* in order to musicalize language in a prolonged way. I like to refer to the result of that process of phonetic abstraction as "language tension" because on the one hand, the chain of alliterations produces difficult-to-define images, interrelating objects our minds would not ordinarily associate and representing a challenge to the reader's thinking. On the other hand, generating a facet or surface opposite the difficulty located in her form, the heart that gives life to the structure of the poems transports us, in a nearly imperceptible way, toward an unfathomable and profoundly moving intimacy:

> I turn around so as not to let your voice go into the void
> of forgotten volumes. I open the fog, I bury you
> in the fog, I give it to you with fog against your tongue
> so your head might hum.
>
> I expose old gooseberries of tumult
> I can hear beneath the fruity mantle of red
> and atop the hypertalky world I open the ramp of my ear
> hypnotized by the mountains of your verbal pupil.
>
> To let you say at length your agglutination
> and put a lurking eye into your scattered
> films. Your film leaves me cold, your film boils
> in my anxiety of attentive ear. (The mute spaces
> are also the graphic screams that accompany us.)

from "(dissections of the bridge)"

The poet thus confronts us with problems of visual association through language; in a symbolic way, these transmit definitions primitively linked to any human being, casting them out toward our understanding. It is in those rare moments within literature that symbols appear, doing their work in a natural way, as before: *before knowing*. And it is that *before* in Laura's language which gives us, at the center of our own language, another idiom. An idiom of our own, as specific as the breathing of the writer herself.

At the two defining extremes of *lobo de labio* — form and depth (which give the impression of opposing one another) — meaning passes by as if it were walking very slowly along a highwire, suspending its significance and, at times, seeming as if it were going to fall without deciphering its *saying*, situating the reader in an irremediable emptiness. This isn't, then, about an ambition to say, it's about the fact that *the saying* appears as the result of a linguistic experience which touches the author's emotional fibers and as a consequence reflects that *I*.

When I understood the true place where Laura has "something" to say, her linguistic structure presented itself to me as a construction determined consciously by its author, unlike the meaning, which sustains form and depth in order to produce the perfection of equilibrium. That equilibrium within tension is what produces the peculiarity specific to *lobo de labio*: the balance between a meticulously sculpted structure and the pulse we cannot see: the *I* of the writer depersonalized by the two extremes drawing each other taut.

At the Margin of the Margin?

Mexico is a country where there is seemingly interminable governmental support for the arts: every year fellowships are given to thirty-five or more artists by each state, and to a hundred and fifty artists by the federal government. The condition for becoming a "fellow" is that the artist must allow her or his proposed project to be directed, for either one year or three years, by artists the government recognizes as "authorities in the field." In this way, homogeneity in the arts is generated in Mexico, since the fellow's style depends principally on the preferences of whoever is acting as the "authority" (I wonder if art can even exist when its creator bows down before authority). There are more than two hundred arts prizes in the country that owe their existence to governmental support.

Government funding has never gone toward supporting what I'll call, just for purposes of definition in this text, "experimental" poetry written by women. Insofar as this support has been given to "experimental" work, it has gone solely to men who work within a mode the "authorities" have denominated "intellectual poetry" and whose books are published in scant quantities and scarcely distributed.

Having made this point clear, I will now dare to claim that Laura Solórzano fulfills all the necessary requirements to be excluded from the governmental apparatus: she's a woman, she's an artist, and she makes risky work that refuses, in its very structure, to account for the judgments of any authority whatsoever. That is, Laura does not write in order to comply with "authority." For that reason, Laura's work is located as "marginal" poetry in our country and (at the same time that it presents us with the beauty of art) it implicitly presents us with resistance to any sacrifice of style in the name of what authority and those who follow it call "tradition." It is, therefore, also a sociopolitical critique of the apparatus that generates official art (though saying *official art* is like saying *institutional revolutionary*: an absolute contradiction, yet it exists):

> To walk within and distract the slope of this profound fall. To compare vices, to void them, to vivify them in the quoin. I'm fretwork you say when you read me? Yours are fauces that don't frequent my fruit. Ficus of infancy beneath a loupe. Your loupe can't see me. It doesn't vanquish my fence with its vision, doesn't encompass (on the slope of fecund fall) the vertebra.
>
> *from "(reading)"*[2]

However, Laura's poetry does not represent a rupture with tradition. Her marginality stems from the work itself, because although Laura does not strictly reproduce a traditional poetics she does assimilate and transform tradition, making use of it and keeping it in movement, concretely alive (the mere reproduction of *what once was* tradition is not tradition).

Contrary to what the "authorities in the field" call tradition, poetry ruled by direct language (because the poet's love-object is her/his reader — as if a Neruda might be born again every year), Laura's poems in *lobo de labio* construct a musical structure, a linguistic vibration so that the emotional and intellectual depth inherent to the human might exist on its own. In *lobo de labio*, Laura demonstrates an enormous concern for self-reflexivity and the exposing of her interior (*there is no poetry without the I*). We should take this to mean the internal, psychological and emotional realm, not the creation of an aggrandized personality exhibited for the scrutiny of others. This is, rather, a truth resulting from constant internal excavation that comes to sustain its own shadows and illuminate them with sufficient acceptance and humility that they become visible, as if the shadows and clarities of others might be illuminated also.

Dolores Dorantes
Ciudad Juárez, Chihuahua
July 2006
Translated by Jen Hofer

1. *Aufgabe* 3 (2003) features contemporary Mexican poetry in translation, with a focus on *Hoja Frugal* (Trans. note).
2. Version published in *Hoja Frugal* 1.3 (Oct. 2001).

7

How to Say What to Say: Translator's Notes

1. Mute Speech, Spoken Speech

> I spell out my house in newly dead tree. I spell out Sunday of clear
> omissions and then languor of a life doubled over and described. Using
> all the letters, I put a strangeness in the coordinates of a suspended
> pain. I spell out this throbbing of eyes open where I would think they'd
> close. Where the bed imposes a palate of months. Letters tend to feel
> another pronunciation, another labial fissure through which they
> emerge savage and happy like unexpected panes of glass.
>
> "Mute Poem," from *Semilla de Ficus.*[1]

Like poetry (but perhaps more insistently), translation puts a strangeness in the
coordinates of our experiences and perceptions. If poetry itself opens eyes unexpectedly, feels
another pronunciation, slices open the not transparent view a pane of glass provides, then
poetry in translation opens eyes that look different than the eyes we expected to have, and
through them ignites us to see differently as well. Poetry in translation pronounces an
unfamiliar feeling that is strange upon our tongue, and it shards open the mirrored view a
reflective glass suggests.

What is accuracy in a landscape of associative double and triple entendres and sonic
acrobatics? How to translate meaningfully into the space of poems where meanings shimmer
between harmonious dissonances and clashing assonances, where senses accrue and
conglomerate exponentially, patterning and unpatterning to the rhythms of an undomesticated
linguistic elasticity trapped within an awareness of the confines of the domestic and the
utterable? The texts in *lobo de labio* are impossible to translate, and therefore the process of
translating them — and the translations themselves — exist entirely in the realm of possibility:
where better for a poet to alight in these days of impossible distress, intellectual and political
duress?

When I say that Laura's poems are "impossible to translate," I do not in the least intend to
invoke the platitudinous write-offs of translation that have infected our general understanding —
or, more accurately, misunderstanding — of the processes and potentialities sparked by the
radically intimate act of reading and writing that is literary translation. I intend, on the contrary
and rather contrarily, to suggest that it is precisely the impossibility of rendering the full syntactic,
musical and denotative complexity of Laura's texts into English that sets up such a strong

foundation for the numerous kinds of possibility outlined by these texts and the processes we explore as we read them and thus rewrite them (translation, as I see it, being principally a form of guided rewriting). The inevitable apertures angling through the congruencies between what Laura has written and what I will write and what you might read are spaces for contemplation and conversation: they are the map of what is possible in this work.

> The voice on horseback. I listen to the breaths, the salivation. I listen to the rapid flow of vowels and consonants, the sonorous eddies of the blood, the coagulation that occasions a state of pause, momentary arrest so as to experience the current of words rotating, unseating old sentences, scratching at the silence to penetrate, to intervene with renewed leverage, the ambiguous mouth and little by little with each letter to advance towards the central approach of their meanings, casually endowed with ungovernable equilibrium.
>
> "Speech Poem," from *Semilla de Ficus.*

Inextricably intertwined and unequivocally incommensurate, the poem (itself an act of translation from experience and perception into language) and its foreign counterpoint (the translation from one language into another) coexist intimately, two expressions of one body — and at the same time, walking toward each other back to back, they know nothing of one another. The translation cannot speak for the original, and it should not, particularly when the languages in question have a long and contested history of interrelation on unequal terms, as is the case with Spanish (a colonized language which in turn is the colonizer of numerous indigenous languages) and English (a colonizing language whose imperialisms create certain kinds of speech, certain kinds of muteness). The translation can speak only for the translation, though the building blocks of its vocabulary may have been developed in another language elsewhere, and its processes invite an unsettling and necessary elasticity into English. Thus the impossibility of translation is the seed of relation and of understanding — and thus of gratitude — occasioned by an encounter with something other than what we already knew how to say.

2. Musicality: Making Meaning Mean

Simplifica (sencillez dorada) el Yo una señal
Silente, al suceder de cimbra en el zumo,
A lo sumo, subo a ver,
Bajo a simplificar,

Simplifies (golden simplicity) the I a silent
Signal, when it occurs swaying in the syrup,
Surely, I ascend to see,
I descend to simplify,

from "(paraiso)"/"(paradise)"

Radically constricted musical impulses like rhyme, assonance and alliteration, to name just a few, tend to stymie translation that would attend to sense as well as sound and sound as integral to sense. Laura's and my copious correspondence about the translations of these poems is filled with my questions to her, her questions to me, our answers to one another which often occasion further questions, and a constant exploration of what makes meaning, and which of a given poem's many levels of meaning the translation should privilege. Laura consistently expresses a preference for sense over sound, as if the two can be separated. Here are some examples of her notes to me:

"The sound isn't so important; the sense is more important, if in fact one can speak of sense."

"I'd prefer that you translate the sense and not the sound, if you have to choose between the two."

"Remember that it's not that I necessarily want to complicate ideas or images; when possible it's better to simplify them. To say things directly and literally, attending to the idea. If the sound is lost, so what."

Translation, in a sense, brings out the literary conservative in me. I realize I believe in meaning and also in meaning's mutability, I believe in authorial intention and also that the author's understanding of a text is just one of many, I believe in denotation as one of the many forms, though certainly not the only form, of the poem's notation. I sincerely want my translations of Laura's texts to provide a window into what those texts say. But what, in this context, is saying? What is said? When Laura's text employs ten or more alliterating words nearly uninterrupted, or a pair of homonyms with radically different meanings ("en el zumo,/A lo sumo" — z and s both sound like s in Spanish), can we pry the sense from the sound and consider the two as distinct categories?

It's no accident, for example, that I replaced Laura's elegantly alliterative-assonant title, *lobo de labio*, with the more prickly, dissonant *lip wolf*, deciding after much conversation that to evoke that particular beast (the wolf) and that particular organ (the mouth, or its entryway, the lip) should take precedence over the sonic chromatism of *lobo de labio*. If writing is faltering into multiple exactitudes, translating is faltering further and more multiply, slipping from image to image, from one realm of resonance to another, with often little possibility for even a glance toward exactitude — as congruence is hardly exact, though it can be, on a good day, exactly inexactly right. Or perhaps it's not about getting it right, but rather about getting into it.

"Zumo" with a z is juice; "sumo" is sum but the idiomatic phrase "a lo sumo" means "at the most." I know Laura's poetics enough to know that when she writes "zumo" she means "juice" and when she writes "a lo sumo" she means "at the most." Of course she recognizes the sonic significance of her phrasing, but despite the often willful misreading of her work as nonsense by the literary powers-that-be in Mexico, Laura is actually more of a literalist than anything else. It is one thing, then, for me to choose to translate the word "subo" as "I ascend" rather than "I go up" to capture the sound of the s — though the registers differ somewhat, the verbs are basically synonymous. Likewise my turning "juice" into "syrup," particularly since "jugo" is the most common word in Spanish for juice and "zumo" can really mean either. "At the most," however, plagued me for months. How in the world could I find a homophone with "juice" or "syrup" that could possibly mean "at the most"? After a few hours of mental wheel-spinning, the phrase "at the most" would cease to mean anything at all to me, and my search for a synonym would then become patently impossible.

There are some moments of doubleness in Laura's writing I simply did not translate. In the poem "(song)," for instance, Laura's line *yo era tímida, un yoyo* teases her timid "I" ("yo") into its own vacillating double, a yoyo. I immediately began playing with opportunities to make an English-language I assent a timid "aye, aye," or somehow roll snake eyes or see double out of an eye and an eye, but I had to concede that nothing yoyos quite like a yoyo, and the "I" in Laura's poem was doing nothing so much as yo-yoing. Convinced that the knots into which I would have to tie the text to reproduce Laura's word-play would do more harm than good to the poem, I settled for the more literal line: *I was timid, a yoyo*. Similarly, I was perhaps not going to get the exact homophony of "zumo" and "sumo" into the English version of "(paradise)," but I wanted to get closer than "juice" and "most," and settled for the possibilities visual and sonic assonance provide rather than continuing to seek an impossible exact homonym.

> ...when it occurs swaying in the syrup,
> Surely, I ascend to see,
> I descend to simplify...

Almost every single poem in *lobo de labio* contains one or many phrases that defy reproduction due to their combinations of sonic and connotative complexity: I could provide numerous examples of my failures in relation to this work, and yawnfully lengthy explications of my decision-making process and choice of words. But why focus on language in this nearly cross-eyed way? As Laura said more than once as I tied myself up in vocabularic knots trying to honor her sophisticated, whimsical, astute, multi-layered use of language — if the sound (or some other element) is lost, so what?

3. Close Listening, Proximate Thinking

In poems an alternate listening opens. In translating listening is honed and expanded, the combined *commune* and *commute* of communication sparking us to link up and move elsewhere, toward spaces that are not familiar but might be kindred instigatory adventures: where better for a poet to alight in these days of impossible distress, intellectual and political duress?

Among many other reasons, I translate to get outside myself and my own writing habits. Working on these poems, I began to write and think like Laura — that is, like the version of Laura these poems reflect, a version of Laura inevitably mediated by me. An example: the first line of poem 12 in the opening sequence of the book reads, in Spanish: *Llenar, ahogar, sembrar, conectar, improvisar en tu luz*. Translated literally, the line would be: *To fill, to drown, to sow, to connect, to improvise in your light*. "Ahogar" (to drown), however, contains within it the word "hogar," home:

a reinforcement of Laura's simultaneous critique of the confines in which domesticity drowns us and her acknowledgment of its generative and connective force. It wasn't exactly a conscious choice on my part to use the word "smother" (containing "mother") instead of drown, but rather an annotation of what I was hearing as I read Laura's poem — that is, what Laura's poems had taught me to hear, my ear tuned to the harmonics of her particular language.

Reading, writing, and translating, at their best, suggest non-normative unconfined modes of listening, and thus congruent modes of conversing. The poem "(affirmation)" claims: *I don't unsay simply to say.* That is: I don't do this to language just to be saying something. And: it's not unsaying that makes this saying. And also: simple unsaying isn't how saying is made. And in addition: what I'm doing is not "unsaying"; it is, simply, to say. *lobo de labio* reminds us viscerally — with its circulatory system of aural annexations and associative propulsions — that *saying* cannot be achieved simply at all. Not by saying, and not by unsaying, but by listening. Via the ear, the attention, the imagination, something can be said and something can be unsaid: to say.

Jen Hofer
Los Angeles, 2006

1. Translations of "Mute Poem" and "Speech Poem" were originally published in *Sin puertas visibles: An Anthology of Contemporary Poetry by Mexican Women*, edited and translated by Jen Hofer (University of Pittsburgh Press and Ediciones Sin Nombre, 2003).

a Federico

Con las imágenes de mi morada
construyo mi lengua y la paso
por cada palabra hasta disimularla en ellas....
(Ana Becciu)

Si no fuese por la flor exterior, que nos mira,
donde volcamos las piedras de nuestras
entretelas, lo oscuro sería un zumbido,
quizás más suave pero inapresable.
(José Lezama Lima)

With the images of my dwelling I construct
my tongue and run it over every word until
it is disguised within them.
(Ana Becciu)

If it were not for the exterior flower, watching us,
where we turn over the stones of our
interiors, the dark would be a buzzing,
perhaps sweeter but ungraspable.
(José Lezama Lima)

1

Decirte cosa, cal, cisterna de cisne subido al despojo
que fragua el césped en tu fobia, frontal e indiferente,
inhóspita y subdividida en cierta acidez, te tengo
anestesiado, sonámbulo de casa de sequedad de severa
insuficiencia, sucia e inyectada.
Tu desliz hacia la forma. Decirte cosa hermosa en la cubierta.
Decirte a ti, tubérculo que trizas el arroz cocido
en el rábano de la salsa insegura, tensas,
tuerces, entierras cal de cisterna de cosa
que se rasca lívida y ligera.

1

To call you thing, cement, swan cistern ascended to the remains
the grass forges in your phobia, frontal and indifferent,
desolate and subdivided in a certain acidity, I have you
anesthetized, dwelling somnambulist of dryness of severe
insufficiency, filthy and injected.
Your slipping toward form. To call you beautiful thing in the slip-cover.
To call you, tuber tearing the cooked rice to shreds
in the radish of insecure salsa, you tauten,
you twist, you inter cement of cistern of thing
scraping itself pallid and light.

2

Decirte materia. Ubicar tu segundo en el aire
que pisa el páramo de tu racimo.
Múltiplos y brotes te baten ciertamente encinta.
Tu pulpa y tu piñata de pelambre pausado.
Cosa de cielo cúbico. Masa, te digo en sopa salada
y sembrada de sorbos. Los arbustos tiemblan.
Silueta verídica que abarcas la carne,
al decirte boca perdida.
Boca de vaca abierta.

2

To call you matter. To locate your second in the air
tread by the terrain of your cluster.
Multiples and buds bombard you positively pregnant.
Your pulp and your piñata of ponderous pelt.
Thing of cubic sky. Dough, I say to you in a salty soup
and sown in sips. The bushes tremble.
Truthful silhouette you comprise the flesh,
when I call you mouth misplaced.
Mouth of cow open.

3

Materia, mordida de hoy sobre la causa tácita.
La masa levanta la deuda y la causa duda física
en el humo, alimentada en la música, masco.
Mastico el cuerpo en el océano de la fábula,
mastico el músculo, miro el monstruo que modera
la esquina. Motivo por el cual muerdo, hoy, amortizo
y muerdo la atadura del origen y la floración de partitura
que viene siendo la firma festiva al inmortalizar.
Muelo en la mesa. Mido.

3

Matter, morsel of today atop the tacit cause.
The dough lifts the debt and the cause doubts physical
in the smoke, nourished on the music, I masticate.
I masticate the body in the ocean of fable,
I masticate the muscle, I watch the monster moderating
the corner. Motive for my nibbling, today, I amortize
and nibble the fastener of origin and the flowering of the score
that comes to be the celebratory signature upon immortalizing.
I mill on the tabletop. I measure.

4

La cosa, intuye la colmena
que habita alrededor del pie en la nube que elevas.
En la posibilidad incorporas cierta tensión
en que te viertes (veraz vaho de tu desierto cabe en mí).
Subo, sorbo, salvo un ejército de niños en la cena,
con una sensación de fosa en casa, secuencias:
el verdadero cielo espía. Te pido raíz en la nube
de un pie, cosa cabal cavando el estallido para ti,
en un cauce de colmena.

4

The thing intuits the beehive
that resides around the foot in the cloud you elevate.
Within possibility you incorporate a certain tension
in which you overturn (veracious vapor of your desert fits inside me).
I ascend, I sip, I save an army of children at supper,
with a sense of hollow in the home, sequences:
the very true sky spies. I ask you for a root in the cloud
of feet, complete thing excavating the explosion for you,
in a beehive channel.

5

Al disolver tu condición de caza, el columpio te acerca
y en la cacería de aquello que te salva, está irte.
Fabricarte un torso significativo
y fornicar hasta quebrar la olla, te toca como casa, cosa.
Quebrada al revés como caverna, este pasto.
Tu ribera de vientos helados y la fogata en los zapatos
transan de noche (al someter al sueño).
Tu tibieza de curva un día se junta en plena disolución.
Quema la cuadra, te cosificas a punto de podar.
Te salvas.

5

When your condition of hunting dissolves, the swing brings you closer
and in the hunt of that which saves you is your leaving.
To fabricate for you a meaningful torso
and to fornicate until the saucepan shatters, that's the task as house, you thing.
Shattered backwards like a cavern, this pasture.
Your shore of frozen winds and the bonfire in shoes
compromise at night (as they submit to sleep).
Your tepidity like a curve one day comes together in full disintegration.
Burns the block, you become a thing at the point of pruning.
You save yourself.

6

Tenerte como si fueras materia,
o rama de materia que escupió el nido.
Nodal, siempre a nado en lo mínimo,
nubosidad de tenaza cuando tendido de tez volcánica
y en la caricia del toldo, tu temor
ha obsequiado su rareza de tránsito.
Comerte, ha sido una sombra en mi penacho,
en mi espátula de querer entrar,
en mi pico de nudos al acecho, tu nuez,
tu conjunto de nuez material o inmerecida,
no ha tenido la nave, el torrente, la travesía
de un tentar pleno, en este pulso de nervios
de negativa que te muerde
desde la médula de mi dedal.

6

To have you as if you were matter,
or a branch of matter the nest spat out.
Nodal, always swimming in the minimal,
cloudiness of pincers when suspended from volcanic complexion
and in the tarp's caress, your terror
has proffered its peculiarity of transit.
To devour you has been a shadow on my crest
on my spatula of wanting to enter,
on my beak of knots on the prowl, your walnut,
your ensemble of walnut, material or undeserved,
has not had the ship, the torrent, the traversing
of touching fully, in this pulsing of nerves
made of negatives that gnaw you
from the marrow of my thimble.

7

Decirte tormenta que ingiere su laguna, libélula
que repasa el pistilo de su enfermedad, decirte de cabeza
y de cutícula, decirte sólo a ti en agua caída,
en relámpagos. Abrir mi pecho para hablar con lanchas
invencibles a tu oreja. Ese pecho, esa barca que se cierra
sobre el lago de la luna, no he sido yo.
Los cables de la noche superan el estrépito que repartes,
te partes donde la lluvia abre la fuente y fundamental,
cae para expresarte un rayo imposible.

7

To call you storm ingesting its lagoon, dragonfly
reviewing the pistil of its illness, to call you of head
and of cuticle, to call you only you in fallen water,
in lightning. To open my chest to speak with invincible
launches to your ear. That chest, that boat closing itself
upon the lunar lake, I have not been.
The night's cables supersede the din you parcel out,
you part yourself where the rain opens the fountain and falls
fundamental to express to you an impossible ray.

8

Decirte cosa otra vez.
Tiempo para sentir y soltarte
para que lo digas tú. Otra vez la espina se pudre intacta
en la penumbra, en un dedo.
Dedo en el dedal dubitativo y deseoso, da la vuelta:
dame el pan para dorar la misa. Muerde,
si quieres que tu frente retoñe, lo que falta es lejos,
es letal, dardo que devora su desliz intermitente y delira
mientras nace, eres tú.

8

To call you thing once again.
Time to sense and to release you
so you will say it. Once again the spine decays intact
in the penumbra, in a finger.
Finger in the doubtful and desirous thimble spins around:
give me the bread to gild the dough. Gnaw,
if you want your forehead to reappear, what's missing is distant,
is deadly, dart that devours its intermittent blunder and is delirious
while it's born, that's what you are.

9

Rajada en el cubo como cicatriz de córnea a la deriva,
iba yo una vez encinta (global en el uso y glútea)
enmarañada de sesos de máscara.
Ese día, di el dado al portador del tiempo y duré más,
cavé mi hoyo a gatas y descendí a la cosa roja
que se muerde en el acto de sacar la gruta por el oído
y duré, duré toneladas de días para llegar a ver mi dádiva.
Deuda durmiente de pestaña, mi maraña humana
comía sesos, y le digo a la cosa hoy, que esta es su casa,
esto cúbico, esta córnea rajada como de cueva oscura.

9

Split apart in the cube like a cornea scar adrift
I was once going along pregnant (global in use and gluteus)
tangled up in brains made of mask.
That day, I gave the dice to the bearer of time and I lasted longer,
I excavated my hollow on all fours and descended to the red thing
gnawing on itself in the act of extracting the cave through the ear
and I lasted, I lasted tons of days to come to see my given gift.
Dormant debt of eyelashes, my human tangle
was eating brains, and I say to the thing today, that this is its house,
this cubic thing, this cornea split apart as if it were a dark cave.

10

Colgar tu risa de ramo en la nubosidad
de ojo inadvertido, de corazón colgante tu cobijo
de jaulas, este remo es río que llamo a raudales de nado,
desprotegida en corazón que roba la hora para hablar,
con ceja, con jardín de juguete, en riel rozas el puente,
como si al completar, como si al callar con carátulas
de mesa misteriosa, madres al arribo y en tu pelo,
o madres de peluche que purifican tu participación,
este influjo y esta jaula, esta jamás vista cuenca
de pupila pendiente, fuera un encuentro entre tú y yo.

10

To hang your branch-like laughter in the cloudiness
of an eye unnoticed, of a heart hanging your haven
of cages, this oar is a river I name in torrents of swimming,
unprotected in heart robbing the time to talk,
with an eyebrow, with a garden of games, on the rail you scrape the bridge,
as if when complete, as if when shushed with clock-faces made
of mysterious tabletop, mothers arriving in your hair,
or plush stuffed mothers who purify your participation,
this influx and this cage, this never seen arroyo
of pending pupil, were to be an encounter between you and me.

11

Llenarte de culebras cansadas, ha sido mi cuerpo.
Llevar el lodo alado, besar de lodazal en la abierta
química. Esta mordaza lúdica no son mis manos,
son, instante ingenuo de tu calca, las desvanecidas
para llenarte de calvas en la selva, llenarte
como lluvia llorosa en tu pulgar de llave maestra.
Entre la hierba puedo cambiar, yacer, mientras te inundo
de llamadas extrañas de extraer la llanura
sobre el horizonte de tu deseo, sobre la gravidez del golpe
y sobre cuerpos, nuestros y cosificados.
Hay que llenarte como a la olla en la llama,
ponerte de fondo físico mi lunar tan otro,
este lugar no es mi cuerpo, este cuerpo no es mi labio.
Te lleno para extraviar el huracán.

11

To fill you with sapped snakes, has been my body.
To bring the winged quicksand, to kiss as quagmire in the open
chemistry. This ludic gag my hands are not,
they are, ingenuous instant of your copy, what has vanished
so as to fill you with bald patches in the forest, to fill you
like tearful rainfall in your master-key thumb.
Among the grasses I can change, rest, while I inundate you
with strange calls of extracting plains
upon the horizon of your desire, upon the pregnancy of the impact
and upon bodies, ours become things.
I have to fill you like the pan in the flame,
to put as your physical background my mole so other,
this place is not my body, this body is not my lip.
I fill you to lure the hurricane astray.

12

Llenar, ahogar, sembrar, conectar, improvisar en tu luz.
Luz de cuna de lobo de labio. Cambiar, para ti,
la quemadura del cántaro. Y al corresponder
a tu cúspide de ahogo, labio tímido, te mido
al llenar, otra vez llenar tu vacío de río de narciso feliz
en la flauta que no cesa. Musicalizar, incorporar tu nevado
al lomo de la muela. Aquí la muela flota, la curva canta,
la cortina celebra su disfraz y tú te juntas.
Colgar, amar, zafar, aventar aquella voz de mamas mansas
en que ríes río, ruedas en la pena púdica de tu texto,
tu tinta de vena que se debate en la llama.

12

To fill, to smother, to sow, to connect, to improvise in your light.
Light of cradle of wolf of lip. To change, for you,
the scald of the carafe. And when I correspond
to your peak of smothering, timid lip, I measure you
as I fill, again to fill your void of river of narcissus happy
in the ceaseless flute. To musicalize, to incorporate your snowfall
at the molar's loin. Here the molar floats, the curve croons,
the curtain celebrates its disguise and you join in.
To hang, to love, to loosen, to chuck that voice of meek mammas
in which you laugh, river, you roll in the prudish pain of your text,
your vein ink that debates itself in the flame.

(movimiento)

No te persigo. No voy detrás de ti para centrarte
en mi pecho de nube efímera o navío de básculas
que se acrecientan sobre el agua. Yo persigo una laguna
de roca intermitente, y en la punta de compuerta te miro
obrar como si en la persecución yo sucumbiera.

No me detengo como aquella vez en que reunida
caí en la mesa de mecer y en toda su brújula de ventisca
enjaulada. No voy de cacería de húmero humeante.
Te pongo en mi recreo de cálculos invertidos. Ya te tengo.

No busco tu regazo para oscurecer el empeño en sí.
El empeño no conoce las formas, celebra su centro
de trama internada en poseerse y se pudre,
lejos de donde podría buscar tu músculo.

No es por ti precisamente esta inundación de tejidos
acalambrados. No es una caja prendida.
No es la luz de tu certeza que estremece la noche.
Esperar a que tu voz se precipite en la compuerta.
Tu vaga voz en la vitrina del viento.
Habrá que esperar a que el reloj te junte.

Mi pulso de pelota ha parido su pauta
(pienso en la pendiente de tus ojos opacos).
La columna vertebral me ha dejado la veta veraniega.
Mi pulso, mi paraguas, mi pintura de pelo,
han escuchado a la pelota parir el ramaje de tu ritual.

(movement)

I don't pursue you. I don't follow behind to center you
in my chest made of ephemeral clouds or ship of scales
that augment atop the water. I pursue a lagoon
of intermittent rock, and at the tip of the hatch I watch you
work as if in pursuit I might succumb.

I don't stop myself like that time when reunited
I fell on the table of tilting and on its whole compass of caged
blizzard. I'm not on a hunt for a vaporous humerus.
I place you in my recreation of inverted calculations. I've got you already.

I don't search for your lap to darken effort itself.
Effort knows no form, it celebrates its center
a plot woven into self-possession and it spoils,
far from where it might seek your muscle.

It's not precisely for you, this flood of cramping
textures. It's not a box turned on.
It's not the light of your certainty that shivers the night.
To wait for your voice to rush to the hatch.
Your vague voice at the wind's shop window.
To wait until the clock collects you.

My polyp pulse has produced its pattern
(I ponder the pitch of your opaque eyes).
This spinal column has left me this summery seam.
My pulse, my parasol, my hair painting,
all have heard the polyp produce the branchings of your ritual.

(laguna)

Justo ahora que compongo la cuarteadura constante,
te he visto cortar, cubrir, culminar en el cauce
como torrente de vino veloz y he confundido
la forma del cristal. Te he querido en la planta,
de pez en el pozo o portavoz en trance.

Pero justo ahora te compongo y te desbaratas,
justo ahora que te cierro de salud en la idea profunda de ti,
encuentro tu recado clavado, tu alambre junto al mío
brotar del muro disuelto.

Justo cuando la luz cegaba nuestras cabezas o carromato
de sobadas sílabas entre dos voces, sedientas suturas
de sonaja distraída en el justo medio, como juncos
en el ombligo del lago (labio letal de lirio perdido
o laguna que mueres en arena).

Justo entonces, cuando las olas anestesiaban la bolsa llena,
cuando las aves se distanciaban en el laberinto,
ese disco gravitó fuera de la secuencia.

La luz cegaba la grava y la gotera se iba girando,
el cromatismo me llevaba a ti, las colmenas, las curvas,
dedos remotos que no han podido contarme.
Vierto la vena que me dejas al lago.

(lagoon)

Just now as I compose this constant quartering,
I've seen you cut, cover, culminate in the trench
like a torrent of swift wine and I have confused
the form of glass. I have loved you in plants,
as fish in the pit, spokesperson in a trance.

But just now I compose you and you disintegrate,
just now as I close you into health in the profound idea of you,
I find your message nailed in, your wire beside mine
bursting from the dissolved wall.

Just when the light was blinding our skulls or junker
of mussed syllables between two voices, thirsty sutures
of rattles distracted just in the exact middle like junkets
in the navel of the lake (lethal lip of lost lily
or lagoon you die in sand).

Just then, when the waves were anesthetizing the full bag,
when the birds were distancing themselves in the labyrinth,
that disc gravitated outside the sequence.

The light blinded the gravel and the gutter was going around,
chromatism took me to you, the hives, the curves,
remote digits that haven't been able to count me.
I void the vein you leave me at the lake.

(báculos)

Te subo a mi lunar, larga lengua, te subo a separar
la sonda del goce de sorda savia y toco la pierna y te grabo,
gradúo la gotera del gancho, engendro un pez,
pinto la oscuridad del clavo, cuadernos
que quiebran su cauda gastando tu gruta.

Yo parto la raíz y en la disección nadas
como si mi lunar fuera una luna llena.
Te orillo a llamar y te lloro al complicar tu música.

Volver al vaso y de vaso vital al cántaro.
La cauda elástica es de cemento, vuelvo
de haber ido al pasado (los pedazos que te veo reunir
son los báculos de tu cerca barbada).
Volver al vértice y a caminar fetal en la matriz,
subo a los ríos como a los verbos de meter la frente
al vaso que nutre. Aquí nos miran mirarnos
y la vulva definida por el dedo diciente da el sitio,
subo a sorbos de lengua.

(batons)

I ascend you to my mole, long-tongued language, I ascend you to separate
the joyous sounding of silent sap and I touch the leg and I engrave you,
I grade the gutter of what grabs you, I engender a fish,
I paint the obscurity of nails, notebooks
that shatter their trail exhausting your grotto.

I split the root and in dissection you swim
as if my mole were a full moon.
I pull you over to call and I cry you to complicate your music.

To venture again to the vessel and from the vital vessel to the carafe.
The elastic trail is made of concrete, I venture
home from having gone to the past (the pieces I see you gather
are the batons of your bearded fence).
To venture again to the vertex and to walking fetal in the womb,
I ascend to the rivers as to verbs sticking their foreheads
into the nourishing vessel. Here they watch us watching ourselves
and the vulva defined by the indicating digit fingers the site,
I ascend to sips of the tongue.

(lectura)

Caminar por dentro y distraer la rampa de su caída
profunda. Cotejar los vicios, vaciarlos, vivificarlos
en la cuña. Ficus de infancia bajo una lupa.
Tu lupa no puede verme. No vence mi cerca con la vista,
no abarca (en la rampa de caída fecunda) la vértebra.

Caminar para distraer la figura sin fe. Felices de férrea
fragancia (fuimos) en el ave de vientos y hoy cabalgo
o tu frecuencia me desconoce al caminar.

Estoy bajo una lupa de cepillos de pelo en la enredadera
del cráneo blanco. Largas lobelias de Lourdes.
Una aliteración en aulas de la niebla. No, nunca, nieve,
nostalgia novelada y navegante.
Estoy bajo una lupa sin ojos.

(reading)

To walk within and distract the slope of this profound
fall. To compare vices, to void them, to vivify them
in the quoin. Ficus of infancy beneath a loupe.
Your loupe can't see me. It doesn't vanquish my fence with its vision,
doesn't encompass (on the slope of fecund fall) the vertebra.

To walk to distract the figure without faith. Felicitous from ferrous
fragrance (we were) in the bird of winds and today I'm on horseback
or your frequency walking does not recognize me.

I am beneath a loupe of hairbrushes within the creeping vine
of the blank cranium. Long lobelia from Lourdes.
An alliteration in the mist's manors. No, never, snow,
nostalgia novelized and navigating.
I am beneath a loupe without eyes.

(señal)

Sentir la soga. Sudar en la monotonía del tentáculo.
No vayas a omitir la soga, ni te salves de la sensación
de sed sedienta. Sírvete al sentir o decir de lirio de ciudad.
Lirios he aprendido de ti, libélulas de labios lechosos.

No vayas a pensar que sólo la pulpa de ansiedad sonaba
en el arroyo. Yo arribaba al sentir la soga y era un sudar.

(Dar el sudor al sol que sabe. Un destino tiembla
en el tumulto al ir sintiendo cómo la sutura nace de gozo
y sobra en el zaguán.)

(sign)

The sensation of the lasso. To sweat in the tentacle's monotony.
Don't omit the lasso now, nor save yourself from the sensation
of thirst thirsty. Serve yourself when you sense or say lilies in the city.
Lilies I've fixed to you, fireflies of lacteal lips.

Don't think that simply the pulp of anxiety sounded
in the arroyo. I was arriving to sense the lasso and it was a sweating.

(To give the sweat to the sun that knows. A destination trembles
in the tumult as it keeps feeling how the suture springs from pleasure
and is surplus in the portal.)

(fusil)

Caer en tu fosa y volver al viento, gama de mundos
oblicuos en cada paso de potencia y en tu forma cerrada,
en esa fábrica frotada, el final se funde y la fosa encalla
en mi cuerpo.

Caer en tu fosa no es caer en mi cuerpo.
Fosa de fauces o fusil de tu labio a mi laguna.

(rifle)

To fall in your grave and return to the wind, gamut of oblique
worlds in each step of strength and in your closed form,
in that frictioned factory, the ending finally fuses and the grave founders
in my body.

To fall in your grave is not to fall in my body.
Grave of gullets or rifle from your lip to my lagoon.

(canción)

Estaba al tanto, tímida y tuya, tanto tiempo
de turbia abierta. Esta silueta es un perderse del entierro
que tapa sin ninguna tensión los tímpanos, hermanos
del tecleo que no se puede obstruir.

Yo estaba al tanto y tenía de todo en el toldo.
Tenía esta cosa sin terreno que parece triturar
cuando se abre el telón. Por ti transitaba,
en ti mi fragua era un temblor atento.
Iba y venía como si no fuera por la voz,
esta valla de vellosidades efímeras.

Luego, seguía tuya en la silla, en la mesa
demolida por los codos encajados como ramas
por debajo, de paso siempre, bajo su albergue grato
y gutural, yo indefinía aún más la espesura.

Abierta en el ojo, abierta en la mesa de mácula
(que no cesa de extender su seducción de aorta)
yo era tímida, un yoyo, una ciruela de cirios
desencontrados y los corazones apretaban
de manera turbia en la abierta.

(song)

I was alert, timid and yours, tons of time
of turbulence opened. This silhouette is a getting lost of the burial
that tamps down with no tension the timpani, siblings
of the finger-tapping that cannot be obstructed.

I was alert and I kept a little of everything in this tarp.
I kept this thing with no terrain that seems to crush
when you open the curtain. Within you I traveled,
in you my forge was an attentive tremor.
I came and went as if it weren't for the voice,
this fence of ephemeral fuzziness.

Later, still yours in my seat, at the table
demolished by elbows inserted like branches
underneath, always incidental, beneath their lodging grateful
and guttural, I undefined the density still more.

Open in the eye, open at the spattered table
(which does not cease to extend its aorta seduction)
I was timid, a yoyo, a plum made of candles
in disagreement and hearts pressing
turbulently against the opened.

(jaspe)

Te desbarato cuando dudo.
Te disuelvo adentro en el vértice.
Veraz vidriera de venas donde suelto el dardo
en la búsqueda. Te tomo de la mano y te llevo,
te empujo continuamente como a una piedra
hacia lo alto de la montaña. Mañana,
me has dicho alguna vez, modera y mantiene
una distracción. Yo batallaba en ti en una duda dada.
No faltaba quehacer. Era un correr de luna que empuja
como yo empujaba en ti la tela en el telar.
Viento que pasaba, puntas que se hendían,
lenguas, siempre ellas y el dedal.
Te desbarato y te empujo. Jalo el jaspe de ti,
mis cabellos me contemplan obrar.

(jasper)

I disperse you when I doubt.
I dissolve you inside in the vertex.
Veracious glassed-in view of veins where I send out a dart
in the search. I take you by the hand and I lead you,
I push you continuously like a stone
toward the top of the mountain. Tomorrow,
you've told me sometimes, moderates and maintains
a distraction. I battled within you inside a predetermined doubt.
There was no lack of tasks. It was a running of the moon pushing
like I was pushing within you the fabric in fabricating.
Wind passing by, tips splitting open,
tongues, always those and the thimble.
I disperse you and I push you. I jerk the jasper of you,
my hair contemplates my construction.

(tránsfugas)

Tenía la hebra en brazos.
Había pestaña en flor y florituras detectadas.
Había pies, plazas, predicamentos: tanto tiempo
que tuve la hebra en la hembra de la mano.
Molía en la mesa. Medía una menstruación, o musicalizaba.
Mecánica mullida en tu sonar, el tictac en el temple
del torso y tinieblas desterradas a cubrir con medicina,
millares de pastillas en el cielo estrellado. Titubeo sí,
tenía la hebra en cinta y a brazadas contemplábamos
el mar. El brío se integraba a la tubería de taberna,
tenedor amado en la tempestad, dosificada en la idea
sentías sonando en la suavidad de guardarla en brazos.

(fugitives)

I held the fiber in my arms.
There was an eyelash flowering and frills detected.
There were paws, plazas, predicaments: tons of time
I held the fiber in the female of my hand.
I milled on the mesa. I measured a menstruation, or musicalized.
Mechanical straw-mound in your sounding, the tick-tock in the temper
of the torso and darknesses outcast to cover with medicine
millions of pills in the star-studded sky. Hesitation, yes,
I held the fiber in a pregnant pause and in armfuls we contemplated
the sea. The vigor was integrated into the tavern tubing,
beloved table in the tempest, dosed out in the idea
you sensed sounding in the softness of keeping it in your arms.

(temporada)

En el pasillo pensante tenía un clavel,
o cosa caída de la falda al pasto de pradera subsiguiente,
como si el sólo seguir fuera la fórmula inventada
por el coro de una experiencia en flor.
Sin hablar de pétalos, los prismas de tus ojos
penaban en la pulsión y por el pasillo que se abría
en la corola, se coronaba la culpa.
De mi vestidura nacían los cuerpos
y los veía pensar en los filamentos de tu perímetro.
Cuerpos de contagio que cumplían cada mañana
un destino inducido. Dar de beber, y dar al brote
su víspera, pasar del corredor al clavel, de la pradera
al precipicio, de la pintura al sol del cuerpo:
cuerpos y cunas que ya se habían conjugado.

(season)

In the ponderous passageway I had a carnation,
or a thing thrown from the skirt to the lawn of a subsequent plain,
as if simply to follow were the formula invented
for the chorus of an experience in flower.
Without speaking of petals, the prisms of your eyes
were pained in the propulsion and along the passageway that opened
in the corolla, culpability was crowned.
Of my clothing bodies were born
and I captured them pondering along the filaments of your perimeter.
Bodies of contagion that comply every morning
with an induced destiny. To offer a bottle and to offer the blooming
its eve, to pass from the corridor to the carnation, from the plain
to the precipice, from the painting in the sun to the body:
bodies and cradles that had already been conjugated.

(tubérculo)

Ubicada en el ébano de la respiración, te sentía.
Tenía un trompo en la uña al sentir.
No como se siente la savia o la sal o el silencio,
sino te sentía titubear exactamente en la tarima del torso.

Un tiro al blanco que vive en Bruselas en vano,
en el viento que se lleva la idea de sembrar a otro sur,
tenía en ti el tenor del sol. El tronco en la uva
de un temor pálido.

Cuando yo lo tenía, tentaba, teniéndolo aún.
Subía la escalera de costuras. Pensaba un tanto aquí,
en el espejo que la luz lapida. La palabra de brea.
La invertebrada.

(tuber)

Located in the ebony of the respiration, I sensed you.
I had a toy top on the fingernail as I sensed.
Not like sap or salt or silence are sensed,
instead I sensed you teetering exactly on the pedestal of the torso.

A shot to the target living in Brussels in vain,
in the wind that whooshes the idea of sowing to another south,
I had in you the tenor of the sun. The trunk on the grape
of a pale terror.

When I had it, I touched it, having it still.
I went up the stairs of sewing. I was thinking a bit here,
in the mirror the light lapidates. The verb made of tar.
The invertebrate.

(ingreso)

Estoy entrando al tiempo, teniendo el tiempo de tierra, entrando a la tempestad del temblor roto en su listón de ocasos y yo entro, torpe turba de pasto, terco peldaño con su abrir de niño que arranca con pies, añosa puesta a secar de días y su sabor en lengua larga de gorjeo. Una laguna como lengua que va entrando a tronar su letargo, que grazna desgranada en la terraza que crepita y contempla. La brizna es un hogar de garzas, un gritar de lodo, una semilla como llave, como llamada que se daña mientras llega a una lluvia imprecisa.

(entrance)

I'm entering time, taking the time of the terrain, entering the tempest of the broken temblor in its strip of sundowns and I enter, torpid turf of pasture, stubborn stair with its child's opening that accelerates feet, aged setting out to dry of days and their taste on the long tongue of gurgling. A lagoon like a tongue going, entering to blast its lethargy, cackling shucked on the terrace that crackles and contemplates. The fiber is a home for herons, a mud bellow, a seed like a key, like a call harming itself while an imprecise rain arrives.

(aparato)

Me llega débil tu voz.
En el aparato de las voces venidas,
la tuya es alta y tambaleante.
Recibo las deudas de tu aviso y sus domesticaciones.
En doblez y dentellada tu voz se invierte, se incrementa
en el vino, se destituye.

Si pudiera tener de ti una voz in vitro, balcones plateados
en tu sien sensible, o cenaduría de pausados planetas
y su verificación en los anaqueles del vocerío.

Cuando lo tenía todo de tu garganta, cuando hablaba
de ti en la bonanza de la calle, cuando era tu voz
lo que tenía, y era tu callo el costal de vertederos insólitos
cuando quieta, cuando insomne, cuando desbarrancada
y me llegaba entre las fauces como la faz del frío,
no había debilidad.

(apparatus)

Your voice reaches me weakly.
In the apparatus of arrived voices,
yours is high and tottering.
I receive the debts of your warning and its domestications.
In duplicity and bite-marks your voice is inverted, increased
in the wine, it is dismissed.

If I might have from you a voice in vitro, silvery balconies
in your tender temple, or a tavern of plodding planets
and their verification in the cupboards of the uproar.

When I had everything from your throat, when I was talking
about you in the street's bonanza, when it was your voice
I had, and it was your callous the sack of uncommon dumping grounds
when quiet, when insomniac, when run off the road
and it reached me among the gullets like the cold's countenance,
there was no weakness.

(seda)

Estoy sombría, sonora sólo en silencio.
Mi cerebro es la zona de un saber sonámbulo,
sueñan repisas en roperos que se enroscan solos.
Solía salir, sacando la solidez como bastón de bestia
o como bajar al suelo sentido, y ahora que salgo
a sacudidas de cielo, sombría en la ciudad,
superada y suelta en la seda de no saber quién sale,
quién surca, cuándo la savia sangra en sudor y cuándo silba.
Estoy como la estancia en el sopor de horas,
como la estancia cuando celebra su tiraje de suelas,
su peldaño, ese solar, ese sacar del zombi la verdadera
cima, y estoy tirando temas sobre la semblanza
de mi soledad, sometida a mí, saturada entre saleros
dispersos con sonrientes diseños.

(silk)

I'm a shady spot, sonorous solely in silence.
My cerebrum is the zone of a somnambulist cognizance,
shelves dream in armoires that twist into curls on their own.
I used to split, extracting solidity like a beast's baton
or like lowering down to the floor, sensitive, and now that I split
shaken out from the sky, shady spot in the city,
surpassed and set loose in the silk of not recognizing who splits,
who sows, when the sap bleeds sweat and when it whistles.
I'm like the sojourn in the stupor of hours,
like the sojourn when it celebrates its run of soles,
its stair, that solar, that extracting from the zombie the true
summit, and I'm throwing themes onto the semblance
of my solitude, subjected to myself, saturated among saltshakers
dispersed with smiling designs.

(barbecho)

Estoy en el plantío, de pie, como pelo de agua,
como gota que se gasta en la pasividad.
Estar en pierna, en patada, en palmera,
en percance clavado. Estoy sembrada,
enterrada en la trifulca, bifurcada
en la terraza de un viejo tensor y sigo en la silla,
sabiendo que escurro de agua. Estoy de planta
en el pinar, conducida hacia un humus de guarida
que hoy gasto aquí, al ganar la guerra de goma.
Se inunda el terreno, se despostilla y me deshojo,
azolve de caída al unísono de la sombra.
Suave el perfume del platanar.
De pantano en pantano, una puerta.
Un tallo que llega, una llamarada en la deidad
de la plántula que apenas brota.
Y entre las semillas llamo a la planta en su paseo,
como llamaría al pie.

(fallow)

I'm in the field, on foot, like a fiber of water,
like a drop dissipating in passivity.
To be on firm legs, on footstep, on palm fronds,
in fixed mishap. I'm sown,
interred in the bellows, bifurcated
on the terrace of an old tensor and I'm still on the seat,
conscious that I'm slippery with water. I'm permanently
in the pine grove, conducted toward a den humus
that today I dole out here, when I win the war of glue.
The terrain gets flooded, gets chipped and I lose my leaves,
silt from the fall in unison with the shade.
Sweet the perfume of the plantain grove.
From swamp to swamp, a door.
A stalk arriving, a flare in the deity
of the plantlet that's barely budding.
And among the seeds I call the plant on its stroll,
as I'd call the foot.

(paisaje)

Si tú volcaras la vista al dúo que dejamos,
volcaras la cerrazón, y salieras a ver, el viento
se ha metido aquí y ha dejado la vuelta a punto
de partir la nube. Siempre él ha trozado el verdadero
bacilo, hilo en boca, rozadura si dejaras de volcar,
si de pronto el poder te negara su puesto de piña,
y así, pisada drástica, sumaras a tu senda de visiones,
los vistazos quemados entre dos.

El deshilado es grave al inhalar de rama en rama tu razón.
Qué razón tenías al roer mi rueda, la rama incisiva encalló
a raudales en tierra de sitio. Y reí al resucitar.
Había enroscado el hilo en tu rabia.

(landscape)

If you were to capsize your gaze toward the duet we desert,
you might capsize obstinacy and come out to watch, the wind
has gotten in here and has left the return about
to divide the cloud. He has always split the actual
bacillus, thread in its mouth, rubbing if you were to cease capsizing,
if suddenly power were to negate you its pineapple position,
and thus, drastic tread, you were to sum up your path of visions,
the glances burnt between two.

The unraveled is sober upon inhaling your reason branch by branch.
What reason you had as you whittled away my wheel, the incisive branch ran aground
in torrents on the terrain of that place. And I laughed as I came back to life.
I had wound the thread up in your rage.

(correo)

Me ha llegado febril tu fe. Tu poderosa fe de amores
en ayuno. Me has llovido tú en la fe de mi fragua
de guiño o frutescencia medicamentosa.
Y no es una fortificación, eres tú que nutres la fresa,
tu facultad de ver me ha dibujado.
Podría hablar más sencillamente a la llovizna.
Más fácil hablar del feto de tu fe
en mi febrero fóbico. No insisto, es simple
saber que sientes y que sobas tu tamaño
en la sustancia, que te subes a la voz
que se fermenta en mí, que yo no te facilito nada,
me fundo en la forma, te invito a ver, invierno de nubes
que reciben de tu vena la creencia o su concatenación.
Cuando me llega, cuando mi flauta es propicia,
tu fe fecunda la máquina de mi roca.

(mail)

Your faith has come to me feverish. Your powerful faith of loves
fasting. You, you have rained me in the faith of my forge
of wink or medicinal frutescence.
And it isn't a fortification, it's you who nourishes the strawberry,
your faculty for sight has drawn me.
I might speak more simply to the drizzle.
Easier to speak of the fetus of your faith
in my phobic February. I don't insist, it's simple
to know that you sense and that you knead your size
in the substance, that you ascend to the voice
that ferments in me, that for you I facilitate nothing,
I found myself in the form, I invite you to see, winter of clouds
that receive from your vein belief or their concatenation.
When I come close, when my flute is propitious,
your faith fertilizes the machine of my rock.

(veladura)

A veces el vuelo bebe de las alas.
A veces el vaho se oscurece en el plasma
y la báscula ha cesado. Momentos
en que veo tu mirar de contagio
y tu pleamar en la mente del cuervo.

Se vence la trama que traías al conjunto.
Se coleccionan, una a una en mi colegio de elementos
transpirados. Y me quedo de pie en la postal
que habla del paisaje, pegada al pesebre
que abre su entrecortado tufo.

Hay otras cuerdas, otros lobos, otros sitios
agarrados al motor, se eleva el motor y así resurjo.
Me bebe el vuelo de tu noche.
Se oscurece la entraña en el venero del vaho.
Es inquietante proceder en el ala, internar el olvido.

(veil)

Frequently flight drinks from wings.
Frequently the fog grows dark in the plasma
and the scale has ceased. Moments
when I see your contagious gazing
and your high tide in the mind of the crow.

It expires, the plot you pulled into the combination.
They collect, one by one in my school of transpired
elements. And I stay standing in the postcard
that speaks of the landscape, linked to the manger
that opens its intermittent fume.

There are other cords, other wolves, other sites
attached to the motor, the motor lifts and so I resurge.
Your nocturnal flight drinks me.
They grow dark, the innards in the fount of the fog.
It's disturbing to proceed on the wing, to intern oblivion.

(libro liviano)

Estoy tan lejos de la losa y su lío.
Linterna de noche cerrada. Me voy metiendo al mundo,
me voy a verte de licor en letargo que alberga el tiempo.
Hoy es tan largo aún. Limbo que mama su mitad de loa,
miedo al musgo, miedo al miedo, locales limoneras
en la noche de linterna empañada.

Tu mirada de muro, la madera de leña.
Yo me alejo al meterme, me alejo tanto que recuerdo
el limo. Mi cavidad de latir, mi labia, mi lecho, mi libar.
Hoy es lugar de leche, lectura de cancel de lejanía,
te hablo del Yo, hablo a la loseta de tu Yo
y libero la lona, leo en tu libro.

Estoy aquí, lunes de labrar que compone
un contexto de letras. Otra vez miedo, otra vez música,
otra lengua ingresa y hoy no siento. Me siento junto a ti,
lirio de sangre de soporte en la mesa, mesero,
estar tan lejos de la losa y su lío, estar contigo.

(trivial text)

I'm so remote from the rock and its ruckus.
Lantern of night closed. I go on winching my way inside the world,
I'll go on seeing you as liquor in lethargy sheltering time.
Today is so drawn out still. Limbo that suckles its section of acclaim,
fear of lichen, fear of fear, lemon-tree locales
in the night of the blemished lantern.

Your wall-like look, wood for fuel.
I remove myself as I move inside, remove myself so far that I'm reminded
of mud. My cavity of pulsing, my labia, my litter, my libation,
today is a moment of milk, partitioned reading of remoteness,
I tell you about the I, I tell you about the little rock of your I
and liberate the linen, I tender your text.

I'm here, monday of making that composes
a context in letters. Once again fear, once again music,
another tongue enters and today I do not feel. I feel myself sitting beside you,
lily of blood borne as a prop at the table, busboy,
to be so remote from the rock and its ruckus, and to be with you.

(paraíso)

Caer de súbito en el sauce,
Abrazar el sauce en la azotea,
Azotar la taza, sangre de taza insólita,
Serpiente, sonido, surco, sorpresa, y sangrar en esto.
Esto siente suyo el ácido, esto trabaja,
Socava junto a ti la quilla
Sopesa y siente la silueta del cerco
Somete, indistintamente la salvación,
Simplifica (sencillez dorada) el Yo una señal
Silente, al suceder de cimbra en el zumo,
A lo sumo, subo a ver,
Bajo a simplificar,
La secuencia que ensaya sonreír, la sensación
Unida al soplo de Silvia,
Inducida como zaguán de sales,
Saliente de zozobra,
En brazos de salva, en selva
De sabueso insolado,
Desfallecer en la falla (hoy llamo al fin)
Solidez (te solvento)
Suposición in situ (salva el sí)

(paradise)

To fall suddenly in the willow,
To embrace the willow on the terrace,
To whip the cup, blood of the uncommon cup,
Serpent, sound, furrow, surprise, and to bleed in this.
This senses the acid is its own, this works,
It excavates the keel alongside you
Weighs and senses the silhouette of the fence
Submits, indistinctly, salvation,
Simplifies (golden simplicity) the I a silent
Signal, when it occurs swaying in the syrup,
Surely, I ascend to see,
I descend to simplify,
The sequence that rehearses smiling, the sensation
United with Silvia's sigh,
Induced like a doorway of salts,
Salient with anxiety
In the arms of a salvo, in the woods
Of a sunstroked sleuth,
To faint in the failure (today I invoke the end)
Solidity (I solve you)
Supposition in situ (save the yes)

(senda)

Si tu cabeza se cansa de caer, si las construcciones cabalgan en tu cuerpo, si no hay calma, ni canasta de calmantes, ni combustión que pueda escuchar tu río.

Si has tenido la sangre en la superficie, si la senda te ha dejado sentado, si la semana te arrastra hacia una sensación, si no hay sensación, si hay silencio.

Si lo que dices suple tu disfraz, si la frase te afrenta, si los huecos conducidos por el rol de sustantivos ahora son verbos, son vasos empapados de verbos y visión.

Podrías traerme a la trampa de mi tierra en tu desliz, tergiversar el tiempo en que tratábamos de entrar y tenerlo ahí, en la tundra intocada.

Podría romper tu rampa, salir del aro de tu rosca y quedar en el resfrío. En la sencillez del rojo, en la rueda pendiente, en el rosal.

(path)

If your head tires of tumbling, if constructions trot on
horseback in your body, if there is no tranquility, nor basket of
tranquilizers, nor combustion that might hear your river.

If you have had blood on the surface, if the path has left you seated,
if the days of the week drag you toward a sensation, if there is no
sensation, if there is silence.

If what you say supplements your disguise, if the phrase affronts
you, if the hollows led by the roll call of nouns now are verbs,
they are glasses soaked by verbs and vision.

You could bring me the trap of my terrain in your slippage, distort
the time in which we tread to enter and have it there, on the
untouched tundra.

I could rupture your ramp, come out from the ring of your coil and
remain in the headcold. In the simplicity of red, in the pending
wheel, in the rosebush.

(cobalto)

Tu cuerpo es concha en el camino del campo. He querido y quiero el fondo de tu cuerpo en la cava de conjuros imparables. Y he pasado el día diciendo cómo y cuánto y qué seduce mi confín. Mi cofia ha dejado de serlo, cobranza de conquista, me digo córnea a la deriva y es un decirte a ti. Cuánto he permitido la caja en ceniza, cuánto perder como si me pudriera en el collar. He tenido tu cuerpo en la cuna, he viajado por la viscosidad como vacío, he comido por codos, al sepultar. Y luego de ver la corpórea razón, ven te digo al querer de cuerpo entero la raíz, la broca despunta en el contorno y despliega su romelia indolora, yo al venir te digo ven, quiero el campamento en la cumbre del cuerpo.

(cobalt)

Your body a conch in the course of the countryside. I have desired and desire the depth of your body in the cellar of unstoppable conjurings. And I have spent the day saying how and how much and what seduces my boundary. My coif has ceased to be that, cashing in of conquest, I call myself cornea adrift and this is a way of calling you. How much I have permitted the box in ashes, how much to misplace as if I were putrefying in the necklace. I have had your body in the cradle, I have traveled the viscosity like a void, I have eaten by elbows as I entomb. And after seeing corporeal reason, come I tell you as I desire whole-bodied the root, the drill bit blunts in the contour and unfurls its painless romelia, when I come, I say to you, come, I desire the encampment at the crest of the body.

(titanio para yáñez)

Puedo esconder mi tinta en el tallo del barco.
El barco de huracán en la pantalla terrible y blanca.
Esconder tu encendedor y eclipsar el puerto de páginas.
El barco se esconde en la tinta del tapiz que termina
virtual, como voluntariosa termita en la madera del temor.
Un tango en alas tuyas, el barco vence su bastión
y lleva tantas bocas, traga el terraplén testigo, te inunda
de tañidos y lo que podría esconder, se derrama
hacia el trastorno (se interesa en ser barcaza de tintura
en la tromba del terreno perdido) y emerge líquida.
No podría esconder el canal de empiezos, con tumba.
Debe abrirse, siempre en labios de agua,
y hablar en los valientes verdes, del barco.

(titanium for yáñez)

I can hide my ink in the boat's stalk.
The hurricane boat on the screen, terrible and white.
To hide your lighter and to eclipse the port of pages.
The boat hides in the ink of the tapestry that ends up
virtual, like a willful termite in the wood of terror.
A tango on wings that are yours, the boat vanquishes its bastion
and brings so many mouths, swallows the embankment witness, floods you
with tolling of bells and what it might hide, spills out
toward the disturbance (is interested in being a tincture barge
in the tornado of lost terrains) and emerges liquid.
It could not hide the canal of beginnings with a tomb.
It must open, always on water's lips,
and speak, in brave greens, of the boat.

(afirmación)

No quisiera extender mi báscula por los abismos
de tu tamaño, ser de astas frías en tu frío. No quisiera
la querencia, tener la caminata y definir la niebla.
No es esto un templo que nació vencido en la niñez
del verbo. No es la luz la verdad en la calmosa anchura
de la noche, no es aquí el caer, no es allá la lluvia,
no hay enfermedad en este crisol de soportes guardados
en garganta.

No vengo a oprimir la melodía en la muela del músico,
tu mirada extiende su silueta y nos parecemos,
nos ofrendamos, nos cogemos del cigoto que crece
al pie del cuento.

Los filos de primavera y la navaja de níveas palmeras,
a finales de invierno. Año clavado en nomenclaturas,
de añicos extraídos, ese diseño de corceles a cuestas,
me ha sucedido acaso en un sueño.

No me desdigo para sólo decir. Ni quisiera ir de domingo
al ras del dolor, capturada en el domo. No es esta la nuez.

Tus flamas de barcaza revuelta se han convertido
en símiles. Tus señales de ocurrencia, de contexto,
de disposición clausurada, tu canica en la cazuela
del placer, tu participación en el círculo
me ha conectado.

(affirmation)

I would not like to extend my scale into the abysses
of your size, to be made of frigid staffs in your freeze, I would not like
liking, to have the walk and to define the fog.
This is not a temple born vanquished in the verb's
childhood. The light is not the truth in the calm expanse
of the night, the falling is not here, the rain is not there,
there is no illness in this crucible of supports guarded
in a gullet.

I haven't come to oppress the melody in the musician's molar,
your watching extends its silhouette and we look alike,
we proffer ourselves, we grab onto the zygote that grows
at the base of the story.

Spring's filed edges and the razors of palm trees snowy,
at the finish of winter. Year fixed in nomenclatures,
of fragments extracted, that design of steed to you yoked
has happened to me perhaps in a dream.

I don't unsay simply to say. Nor would I like on a Sunday
to go on a par with soreness, captured in the cupola. This is not the nut.

Your jumbled barge flames have turned
into similes. Your signs of occurrence, of context,
of disposition shut down, your jacks in the casserole
of pleasure, your participation in the circle
has connected me.

(decantar)

Me gusta ver tu línea de manos, liberar el lago.
Me gusta tu conexión tardía en la ruta de estrepitosas
romerías. Tu asombro es bosque de cazas, de rupturas
en recinto más allá del acceso. Mi acceder sólo a tu rodilla,
dinamita o dátil, en la despensa de la buena señal.

(Hablo de ver de bulto y en mi boa de verano,
basta la visión.)

Si la llamarada se ha perdido, si la insistencia ha caminado,
si la viruela te ha introducido la comezón de la noche,
habrá que pedir salud al péndulo que domina la voz.

Tú y la voz de batalla.
La planicie y los escuderos de la voz.
Porque mi barca te cerca.
Mi basura te busca.
Mi comezón termina su tatuaje a cierta edad.

Voy a poner la planta en la pena de perder el peral.
Y nunca sabrás cuánto me gustan las líneas de tu lago
en la mano ilusoria. Cómo me gusta la creación
de tu conectar a gajos de cal.

Deseo doblar, deseo durar en lo tuyo que reparte
y sostiene esta vagancia. Por eso voy de boca,
voy al lago, vengo a caer en ti.

(to decant)

I like to see your line of hands liberate the lake.
I like your tardy connection along the route of boisterous
pilgrimages. Your astonishment is a forest of hunts, of ruptures
in enclosure beyond access. My acceding only to your knee,
dynamite or date, in the pantry of the good sign.

(I speak of seeing in bulk and in my boa of summer,
vision is enough.)

If the flare has been lost, if insistence has walked,
if smallpox has introduced you to itching in the night,
it will be necessary to ask the pendulum that dominates the voice for health.

You and the voice of battle.
The plain and the shieldsmen of the voice.
Because my boat fences you.
My trash searches for you.
My itch terminates its tattoo at a certain age.

I am going to put the plant in the pain of misplacing the pear tree.
And you'll never know how much I like the lines of your lake
in the illusory hand. How I like the creation
of your connecting in segments of cement.

I want to double, I want to endure in what is yours which distributes
and sustains this vagrancy. That's why I go from the mouth,
I go to the lake, I come to fall in you.

(ánimas)

Ando en el contexto de tu esquina,
ando en almas claras de cursivas incautas.
Ardo sobre la andadera de tu mano y en arpegios
desolados al abrigo del golfo me digo en semilla,
digo en máquinas, me detengo en deleite de musa
voy a nado en médanos al navegar en vistas blancas
devoradas de negro en el trabajo de pensar.

Y si el contexto ampara el andén de tu cara y si la textura
se aviene a la ventura de tu halo, la andanza que destina
su alubia será tuya, la andanza sabrá comparecer y la idea
que por tu mano alivia el cazo, suscitará el amor.

(animas)

I wander in the context of your corner,
I wander in clear spirits of incautious italics.
I flare upon the wanderlust of your hand and in arpeggios
desolate within the harboring of the gulf I say myself in seeds,
I say in machines, I'm detained in muse delight
I wander water in dunes as I navigate in white vistas
devoured by black in the work of thinking.

And if context protects the platform of your face and if texture
adapts to the happenstance of your halo the occurrence that destines
its beanstalk will be yours, the occurrence will know to make its appearance and the idea
that by your hand alleviates the vessel, will occasion love.

(disecciones del puente)

Doy la vuelta, para no dejar ir tu voz al vacío
de los volúmenes olvidados. Abro la bruma, te interno
en la bruma, te doy con la bruma en la lengua
para que tu cabeza cante.

Expongo viejas grosellas de tumulto,
que puedo escuchar bajo el manto frutal del rojo
y sobre el mundo hiperparlante abro la rampa de mi oreja
hipnotizada por las montañas de tu pupila verbal.

Dejarte decir de largo tu aglutinamiento
y poner un ojo que acecha en tus desparramadas
películas. Tu película me deja fría, tu película hierve
en mi ansiedad de oído atento. (Los espacios mudos
son también los gritos gráficos que nos acompañan.)

Cada músculo del vendaval se nutre de mi espera
de párpado extasiado. Cada letra de tu agarrar es voz
subiendo su escalera predilecta. Cada cicatriz de ti
en mi orificio auditivo es una flor de suspenso.

Te escucho porque albergo mil pedazos
que palpan un cerebro interior. Cerebro de hielo
que se funde bajo un cristal conjugado.
Es inútil cerrar el receptor.

Mi receptor es vida que mueve su retícula
para alcanzar su parte de ingreso. Dejar que ingrese
el rojo labor de tu tránsito y abrazada a la paráfrasis vital,
sentirte acceder.

(dissections of the bridge)

I turn around so as not to let your voice go into the void
of forgotten volumes. I open the fog, I bury you
in the fog, I give it to you with fog against your tongue
so your head might hum.

I expose old gooseberries of tumult
I can hear beneath the fruity mantle of red
and atop the hypertalky world I open the ramp of my ear
hypnotized by the mountains of your verbal pupil.

To let you say at length your agglutination
and put a lurking eye into your scattered
films. Your film leaves me cold, your film boils
in my anxiety of attentive ear. (The mute spaces
are also the graphic screams that accompany us.)

Each muscle of the gale wind is nourished by my wait
of ecstatic eyelid. Each letter of your grasping is a voice
ascending its preferred staircase. Each scar of you
in my auditory orifice is a flower of suspense.

I hear you because I shelter a thousand pieces
that grope an interior cerebrum. Cerebrum of ice
melting beneath a conjugated looking-glass.
It's useless to close the receptor.

My receptor is life moving its reticulum
to achieve its part of the entrance. To allow the red
labor of your transit to enter and in vital paraphrasing's embrace
to feel you acceding.

*

¿cuál es el rostro que roza mi rueda?
¿cuál es la rima que rodea la razón, quién roba?
¿a quién robarle el remo?
¿con cuál amor rascas inútil en riscos de rapiña?
¿con quién restas, cuál reino y qué ritual?
¿cuál es el respiro que rasga el ropero al retrasar
la reuma? ¿ríes?
¿rieles en tu risa de ramillete erizado?
¿el ramaje lo recuerda? ¿como el recital?
¿si tu rostro dejara el rastro, si tu erupción
argumentara el rotavirus, si el rimmel rajara?
¿en qué rincón, con qué resorte?

*

which round face grazes my wheel?
which rhyme surrounds reason, who robs?
from whom to rob the oar?
with what amorousness do you uselessly scrape at crags of prey?
with whom do you remain, which realm and which ritual?
which respiration rips the armoire as it retards
the rheumatism? your laughter?
rails in your grin of bristling arrangement?
the branching remembers it? like the recital?
if your round face might leave a trace, if your eruption
might argue the rotavirus, if the mascara might crack?
in which corner, with which coil?

*

¿cuál es el rostro ambientado en la duda?
¿cuál es la dirección? ¿cuál deseo, en qué doblez invertir?
¿si el rostro se durmiera en la docencia del dominio,
cuál sería el rodapié dorado?
¿qué decir, cuánto durar, en qué danza?
¿cuál disfunción, me hubiera dado qué? ¿en qué diente?
¿dónde es la duna y dónde el disco?
¿la dosis del yo?
¿una deuda, una dalia?

*

which is the face surrounded by doubt?
which is the direction? which desire, in which duplicity to invest?
if the face were to dream in the educating of dominion,
which would be the gold-burnished baseboard?
what to say, how long to endure, in which dance?
which dysfunction, would have handed me what? on which tooth?
where is the dune and where the disc?
the dose of the I?
a debt, a dahlia?

*

¿quién tercia en el triángulo? ¿quién tantea?
¿cuándo tocar la textura y dejar la lengua en trance?
¿es trueno de lámparas impasibles bajo el amparo
de trémula que te ciñe? ¿es un vuelco en la tapia
del temor? ¿pero el placer es tuyo?
¿quién integra el tapiz? ¿quién tiembla en la torre?
¿la tempestad se anida y tiembla, a quién tocar
en el tendón incompleto?
¿largo y luminoso tendón de lima tendida?
¿quién eres tú? ¿cuál tensor? ¿cuál tripa de química?

*

who participates in the triangle? who scrutinizes?
when to touch the texture and leave the tongue in a trance?
is it thunder of impassible lamps beneath the shelter
of trembling that encircles you? is it a tumble in the adobe wall
of terror? but the pleasure is yours?
who integrates the tapestry? who trembles in the tower?
the storm nests and trembles, whom to touch
in the incomplete tendon?
long and luminous tendon of extended lime?
who are you? which tensor? which chemical entrail?

*

¿sabes del sudor, eres la silla en la sien, la sanidad velada
y sangras, te saluda el ojo y te incendia?
¿sabes del sueño sumergido en el sobre?
¿tu soledad? ¿tu sal? ¿selva de sales secretas?
¿y luego del salto, luego en lo fijo del sol? ¿te suplo?
¿te sostengo en la ese? ¿te siento en sonidos? ¿eres el sopor?
¿sacas la silueta en la calle del soplo sólido?
¿sabes y sigues? ¿sostienes como circo, la sustancia en la lumbre?
¿te sustraigo al salir? ¿silenciosamente escuchas? ¿la pura sensación?

*

you're an expert in sweat, you're the seat at the side of the head, hidden health
and you spill blood, the eye sends you a salutation and incites you?
you're an expert in sleep submerged in a missive?
your solitude? your salt? swamp of secret salts?
and later, after the fall, later in what the sun has fixed? i substitute you?
i sustain you in the s? i sense you in sounds? you're the stupor?
you extract the silhouette on the street of the solid gust?
you're expert and you ensue? you sustain like a circus, substance in the glow?
do i subtract you when i slip away? silently you listen? pure sensation?

*

¿vienes a la voz? ¿viajas por venir al berro?
¿vuelves, a bocanadas de avestruz? ¿este velamen es tuyo?
¿vas a volcar el Vesubio como vena vieja
o vienes a vernos? ¿vigente?
¿biselado en volumen imberbe? ¿es esto el vino?
¿veloz centella? ¿veloz camelia? ¿velocípedos de ti?
¿vienes a verme en la verdura verdadera,
como si mi alimento volara?
¿ves el viaje venir al curul y contemplas la veladura?
¿y si el verdor versificara? ¿eres vaho?
¿vaho de valientes vibraciones?

*

do you arrive at the voice? do you voyage to arrive at watercress?
do you return, in swallows of ostrich? these sails are yours?
will you overturn Vesuvius like vintage vein
or do you arrive to view us? in vogue?
beveled in beardless volume? is this the wine?
swift spark? swift camellia? velocipedes of you?
do you arrive to view me in the veracious verdure,
as if my food might fly?
do you view the voyage arriving at the curule and contemplate the varnish?
and if the verdancy were to versify? are you vapor?
vapor of valiant vibrations?

*

¿te acercas a mirar el monte de mugre?
¿te acercas a la mugre sin dimensión, te doblas en mural?
¿te vas hundiendo? ¿vas domesticando decibeles
de madera? ¿de dulce? ¿ardes en la tela?
¿antepones la dolencia, te vas como vienes sin llegar?
¿te dosifican? ¿eres mínima dosis? ¿te dan el dedo?
¿cuál es el dedo para darte el panal?
¿te detienes a mirar el monte?
¿te vas manchando de moscas en la muralla que masca?
¿la madriguera de indecisiones está dentro de ti?

*

do you approach to watch the mountain of grime?
do you approach the grime without dimension, do you double in the mural?
do you go sinking? do you go domesticating decibels
of wood? of candy? do you burn on the cloth?
do you put pain first, do you go like you arrive without getting there?
do they dose you? are you a minimum dose? do they donate the finger to you?
which is the finger for donating the honeycomb to you?
do you wait to watch the mountain?
do you go blemishing yourself with flies on the masticating rampart?
the den of indecisions is inside you?

*

¿cómo pensar en tu destino?
¿pasar por el péndulo de la patraña en la punta?
¿apuntar, tú y yo? ¿pasar de largo en piedras?
¿pavimentos en tu pelo de improbables?
¿poner paja? ¿tu paladeo? ¿tu para atrás?
¿tu pezón de pus?
¿cuánta pirueta persiste en tu pastilla?
¿cuánto has pedido en el plato?
¿la pausa ocupa la pena?
¿la pena opaca?

*

how to ponder your destiny?
to pass through the pendulum of the prevarication on the point?
to point out, you and I? to pass at length on pebbles?
pavements in your hair of improbabilities?
to place straw? your savoring? your being behind?
your pus nipple?
how much pirouette persists in your pill?
how much have you petitioned on the plate?
the pause occupies pain?
pain eclipses?

*

¿abierta, te alzas?
¿aérea, como aro de ave te alzas en árboles de asombro?
¿te ampara el adverbio? ¿te abraza el páramo del artículo?
¿te aleja el hiperactivo verbal del hecho?
¿no tienes hechura? ¿no hay hinchazón en el aura?
¿es alma y músculo y molécula?
¿el núcleo en la erosión del arco?
¿se aleja, te afrenta, te alaba el ardor?
¿te alzas en el ártico del amor, como arcángel domado?
¿te drogas? ¿te doblega el delirio del descuido,
te duplicas, en la disolución del ámbar?
¿del ámbar hambriento?

*

agape, you ascend?
aerial like an avian arrow you ascend in aspens of amazement?
and the adverb gives you asylum? the wilderness of the article accepts you?
and the hyperactive verbal actually alienates you?
are you impossible? is there not inflation in your aura?
is it anima? muscle? molecule?
the nucleus in the erosion of the arc?
and ardor draws away and affronts you and acclaims you?
and you ascend in the amatory arctic as a golden archangel?
are you on drugs? does the dominion of disregard destabilize you,
do you double, is this the dissolution of amber?
the ravenous amber?

(fin)

Ya no quiero tu cordón,
ahora la costura de contacto va consciente y sola.

Hay entre las palabras una llanura de silla, que no cabe.
Hay entre tus pestañas un marcapasos entristecido,
como de yegua sin llano.

Tu cuerda me ha definido favorablemente porque fija
el camisón, pero tu guiño engarzado a la góndola, golpea.

Hay entre tus manos una manzana de mímica oprimida
como un largo viaje de cejas al vaivén verde
y maniatado del vocablo.

Ya no quiero tu cuerda, quiero el canasto colaborador
para decir en el colegio del pasado, la calle entera.

Hay algunos números inmisericordes entre cabezas
nerviosas y cierta sensación de llamarada
de ayeres en llanto.

Quiero un cofre sin carencia en la ciudad de tu sangre.

(end)

I don't want your cordon anymore,
now the needlework of contact continues conscious and alone.

There is between words a chair-like evenness that doesn't fit.
There is between your eyelashes a saddened pacemaker,
as of a mare with no prairie.

Your cord has defined me favorably because it fastens
my nightgown, but your wink mounted to the gondola strikes blows.

There is between your hands an apple of oppressed mimicry
like a long journey of eyebrows to the oscillation, green
and shackled to the word.

I don't desire your cord anymore, I desire the collaborating container
to say the entire street in the college of the past.

There are some merciless numbers between nervous
heads and a certain sensation of the blazing
of yesterdays sobbing.

I want a coffer without lack in the city of your blood.

(final)

Ya no te abro de pinceles ligeros,
ahora clavo el pino más alto en tu invernadero.
Ya no te quiero en el quiste de cartón, entre conjuntos
irisados por montañas.

Ahora cunde mi cuaderno, corto el papel en pliegues
de cordura de caballo cansado. Se cansa el callejón
y se inquieta en el pilar de tu vacío.

Ya no te abro en brazos, ahora bordo con la barba
de vencer la suavidad del ganso y es un gobierno de cisnes
que observan mi boca.

Ahora te nado, ahora te anudo,
ahora es sólo un decir de viento que vibra en el volcán.
Porque ya no te planteo la posición de la semilla,
ya no te modifico en la tina de saberte teñido, y no es
abrirme a las palabras sino cerrar el cúmulo en calma.

Ahora que te interno en el pasto,
esta calma de cuaderno se compromete a cavar.

(ending)

I no longer broach you with light brushstrokes,
now I spike the highest pine in your hothouse.
I no longer cherish you in the cardboard cyst, between iridesced
groupings of mountains.

Now my notebook snowballs, I cut the paper in pleats
of sageness of spent stallion. The alleyway is spent
and agitated in the basin of your emptiness.

I no longer broach your embrace, now I embroider with the barb
of conquering the soft of the goose and it's a government of swans
who observe my mouth.

Now I snorkel you, now I knot you,
now it's just a saying of the wind vibrating in your volcano.
Because I no longer propose the seed's position for you,
I no longer modify you in the tub of knowing that you're tinted, and it's not
opening myself to words but rather closing the cumulus calmly.

Now that I intern you in the pasture,
this notebook's calm commits itself to excavate.

Acknowledgments

Some of these translations have been previously published in *Action Yes* #2 (http://actionyes.org/issue2/solorzano/solorzano1.html), *Aufgabe* #3, *Bombay Gin* #32, and *Fascicle* #2 (http://www.fascicle.com/issue02/translations/solorzano1.htm). Thanks to Johannes Göransson, Joyelle McSweeney, and John Dermot Woods; E. Tracy Grinnell; John Sakkis; and Tony Tost respectively for their support of this work.

Unflagging gratitude for the friendship and brilliant thinking of Dolores Dorantes, Patrick Durgin, Anna Moschovakis and Mónica de la Torre. **(JH)**

My gratitude to Jen for her willingness to delve into this text so meticulously, to Dolores for her careful observations about language, to Garrett for having been there, to Johannes and Joyelle for taking this risk, to Jorge for his encouragement and confidence in me, and to my kids for putting up with my silence in front of the computer. **(LS)**

Bios

Laura Solórzano was born in Guadalajara, Jalisco in 1961. She is the author, most recently, of *Boca perdida* (bonobos, Metepec: 2005), *lobo de labio* (Cuadernos de filodecaballos, Guadalajara: 2001) and *Semilla de Ficus* (Ediciones Rimbaud, Tlaxcala: 1999). She is on the editorial board of the literary arts magazine *Tragaluz*, and currently teaches writing at the Centro de Arte Audiovisual in Guadalajara.

Jen Hofer moved to Los Angeles from Mexico City in 2002. Her recent publications include *Sin puertas visibles: An Anthology of Contemporary Poetry by Mexican Women* (University of Pittsburgh Press and Ediciones Sin Nombre, 2003), *slide rule* (subpress, 2002), and the chapbooks *laws* (dusie e-chap, 2006) *lawless* (Seeing Eye Books, 2003) and *sexoPUROsexoVELOZ* (translations of poetry by Dolores Dorantes, Seeing Eye Books, 2004). Her next books will be a full-length translation of Dorantes' *sexoPUROsexoVELOZ*, forthcoming from Kenning Editions, *The Route*, a collaborative epistolary and poetic correspondence with Patrick Durgin (Atelos, 2007), and a book-length series of anti-war-manifesto-poems, titled *one*, forthcoming from Palm Press.

2006/2007 Action Books Titles

you are a little bit happier than i am by Tao Lin
Winner of the 2005 December Prize
ISBN: 0-9765692-3-X
ISBN: 978-0-9765692-3-7

Telescope by Sandy Florian
ISBN: 0-9765692-4-8
ISBN: 978-0-9765692-4-4

You go the words by Gunnar Björling, translated by Fredrik Hertzberg
Scandinavian Series #2
ISBN: 0-9765692-5-6
ISBN:: 978-0-9765692-5-1

The Edge of Europe by Pentti Saarikoski, translated by Anselm Hollo
Scandinavian Series #3
ISBN: 0-9765692-6-4
ISBN: 978-0-9765692-6-8

lip wolf by Laura Solórzano translated by Jen Hofer
ISBN: 0-9765692-7-2
ISBN: 978-0-9765692-7-5

2005 Action Books Titles

The Hounds of No by Lara Glenum
ISBN:0-97656592-1-3

My Kafka Century by Arielle Greenberg
ISBN:0-97656592-2-1

Remainland: Selected Poems of Aase Berg,
translated by Johannes Göransson
Scandinavian Series #1
ISBN:0-97656592-0-5